My HOLY HOUR
St. Veronica

A Devotional Journal

Season: _____
Date: _____

Belongs to: _____

My Holy Hour - St. Veronica is part of the *My Holy Hour Devotional Journal Series.* While all journals will have some similar structure and intent, each one will have minor changes to make it unique. Cover image depicts The Resurrected Christ.

Go to our website for a free copy of
How to Use a Prayer Journal during Holy Hour
www.HolyHourBooks.com

Holy Hour Books
P.O. Box 430577
Houston, TX 77243

My Holy Hour Devotional Journals

Copyright © 2017 Vikk Simmons
All rights reserved worldwide

Cover Image by Zatletic/Bigstock
(Saint Veronica wipes the face of Jesus)

ISBN-13: 978-1-941303-34-4
ISBN-10: 1-941303-34-X
First Printing: March, 2017

Holy Hour Books is an imprint of Ordinary Matters Publishing.

All rights reserved. No part of this book may be reproduced in any form or by any electronic or mechanical means, including information storage and retrieval systems, without permission in writing from the author, except in the case of brief quotations used in critical articles or reviews. This means that you cannot record or photocopy any material, ideas, or tips that are provided in this book. Requests for permission should be addressed to the publisher.

Printed in the United States of America

Why Keep a Holy Hour

"First, the Holy Hour is not a devotion; it is a sharing in the work of redemption... our Lord asked: 'Could you not watch one hour with Me?'. In other words, he asked for an hour of reparation to combat the hour of evil; an hour of victimal union with the Cross to overcome the anti-love of sin.

Secondly, the only time Our Lord asked the Apostles for anything was the night he went into his agony... As often in the history of the Church since that time, evil was awake, but the disciples were asleep. That is why there came out of His anguished and lonely Heart the sigh: 'Could you not watch one hour with me?' Not for an hour of activity did He plead, but for an hour of companionship.

The third reason I keep up the Holy Hour is to grow more and more into his likeness. As Paul puts it: "We are transfigured into his likeness, from splendor to splendor.' We become like that which we gaze upon. Looking into a sunset, the face takes on a golden glow. Looking at the Eucharistic Lord for an hour transforms the heart in a mysterious way as the face of Moses was transformed after his companionship with God on the mountain. Something happens to us similar to that which happened to the disciples at Emmaus. On Easter Sunday afternoon when the Lord met them, he asked why they were so gloomy. After spending some time in his presence, and hearing again the secret of spirituality - 'The Son of Man must suffer to enter into his Glory'" - their time with him ended and their "hearts were on fire." — Bishop Fulton Sheen

My Holy Hour

How to Keep a Holy Hour

"I have found that it takes some time to catch fire in prayer. This has been one of the advantages of the daily Hour. It is not so brief as to prevent the soul from collecting itself and shaking off the multitudinous distractions of the world. Sitting before the Presence is like a body exposing itself before the sun to absorb its rays. Silence in the Hour is a tete-a-tete with the Lord. In those moments, one does not so much pour out written prayers, but listening takes its place. We do not say: 'Listen, Lord, for Thy servant speaks,' but 'Speak, Lord, for Thy servant heareth.'" — Bishop Fulton Sheen

"Know also that you will probably gain more by praying fifteen minutes before the Blessed Sacrament than by all the other spiritual exercises of the day. True, Our Lord hears our prayers anywhere, for He has made the promise, 'Ask, and you shall receive,' but He has revealed to His servants that those who visit Him in the Blessed Sacrament will obtain a more abundant measure of grace." — St. Alphonsus Liguori

My Holy Hour

Holy Hour Pages

"The purpose of the Holy Hour is to encourage deep personal encounter with Christ."

— Bishop Fulton Sheen

My Holy Hour

My Holy Hour

My Holy Hour

My Holy Hour

My Holy Hour

My Holy Hour

My Holy Hour

My Holy Hour

My Holy Hour

My Holy Hour

My Holy Hour

My Holy Hour

My Holy Hour

My Holy Hour

My Holy Hour

My Holy Hour

My Holy Hour

My Holy Hour

My Holy Hour

My Holy Hour

My Holy Hour

My Holy Hour

My Holy Hour

My Holy Hour

My Holy Hour

My Holy Hour

My Holy Hour

My Holy Hour

My Holy Hour

My Holy Hour

My Holy Hour

My Holy Hour

My Holy Hour

My Holy Hour

My Holy Hour

My Holy Hour

My Holy Hour

My Holy Hour

My Holy Hour

My Holy Hour

My Holy Hour

My Holy Hour

My Holy Hour

My Holy Hour

My Holy Hour

My Holy Hour

My Holy Hour

My Holy Hour

My Holy Hour

My Holy Hour

My Holy Hour

My Holy Hour

My Holy Hour

My Holy Hour

My Holy Hour

My Holy Hour

My Holy Hour

My Holy Hour

My Holy Hour

My Holy Hour

My Holy Hour

My Holy Hour

My Holy Hour

My Holy Hour

My Holy Hour

My Holy Hour

My Holy Hour

My Holy Hour

My Holy Hour

My Holy Hour

My Holy Hour

My Holy Hour

My Holy Hour

My Holy Hour

My Holy Hour

My Holy Hour

My Holy Hour

My Holy Hour

My Holy Hour

My Holy Hour

My Holy Hour

My Holy Hour

My Holy Hour

My Holy Hour

My Holy Hour

My Holy Hour

My Holy Hour

My Holy Hour

My Holy Hour

My Holy Hour

HOLY HOUR QUOTES

"Thou hast said, 'Seek ye my face.' My heart says to thee, They face, Lord, do I seek." — Psalm 27:8

"And the King will answer them, 'Truly, I say to you, as you did it to one of the least of these my brethren, you did it to me.' Then he will say to those at his left hand, 'Depart from me, you cursed, into the eternal fire prepared for the devil and his angels; for I was hungry and you gave me no food, I was thirsty and you gave me no drink, I was a stranger and you did not welcome me, naked and you did not clothe me, sick and in prison and you did not visit me.' Then they also will answer, 'Lord, when did we see thee hungry or thirsty or a stranger or naked or sick or in prison, and did not minister to thee?' Then he will answer them, 'Truly, I say to you, as you did it not to one of the least of these, you did it not to me.' And they will go away into eternal punishment, but the righteous into eternal life."— Mathew 25:40

"Your Face, O Lord, I seek": "seeking the Face of Jesus must be the longing of all of us Christians; indeed, we are 'the generation' which seeks his Face in our day, the Face of the 'God of Jacob.' If we persevered in our quest for the Face of the Lord, at the end of our earthly pilgrimage, he, Jesus, will be our eternal joy, our reward and glory forever."— Pope Benedict XVI

"May the Lord bless you and keep you: may the Lord make his face to shine upon you and be gracious to you: may the Lord lift up his countenance upon you and give you peace. Amen!"—Numbers 6:24-26

My Holy Hour

Record Your Favorite Quotes Here

My Holy Hour

My Holy Hour

My Holy Hour

My Holy Hour

REFLECTIONS

My Holy Hour

My Holy Hour

My Holy Hour

Personal Index

_____ Pgs ____

_____ Pgs ____

_____ Pgs ____

_____ Pgs ____

_____ Pgs ____

_____ Pgs ____

_____ Pgs ____

_____ Pgs ____

_____ Pgs ____

_____ Pgs ____

_____ Pgs ____

My Holy Hour

_____ *Pgs* ____

_____ *Pgs* ____

_____ *Pgs* ____

_____ *Pgs* ____

_____ *Pgs* ____

_____ *Pgs* ____

_____ *Pgs* ____

_____ *Pgs* ____

_____ *Pgs* ____

_____ *Pgs* ____

_____ *Pgs* ____

_____ *Pgs* ____

HOLY HOUR JOURNALS

Thank you for your interest in *Holy Hour Journals*. Discover more about using journals to deepen your prayer life by going to our website and getting a free copy of

How to Use a Prayer Journal during Holy Hour
www.HolyHourBooks.com

The Holy Hour Devotional Journal Series has been created to help Catholics from all walks of life to discover, explore, and enjoy the many rewards from a deeper connection to Christ.

Like our Facebook Page:
https://www.facebook.com/HolyHourBooks

Made in the USA
Lexington, KY
19 April 2018